INSULTS
COLORING BOOK

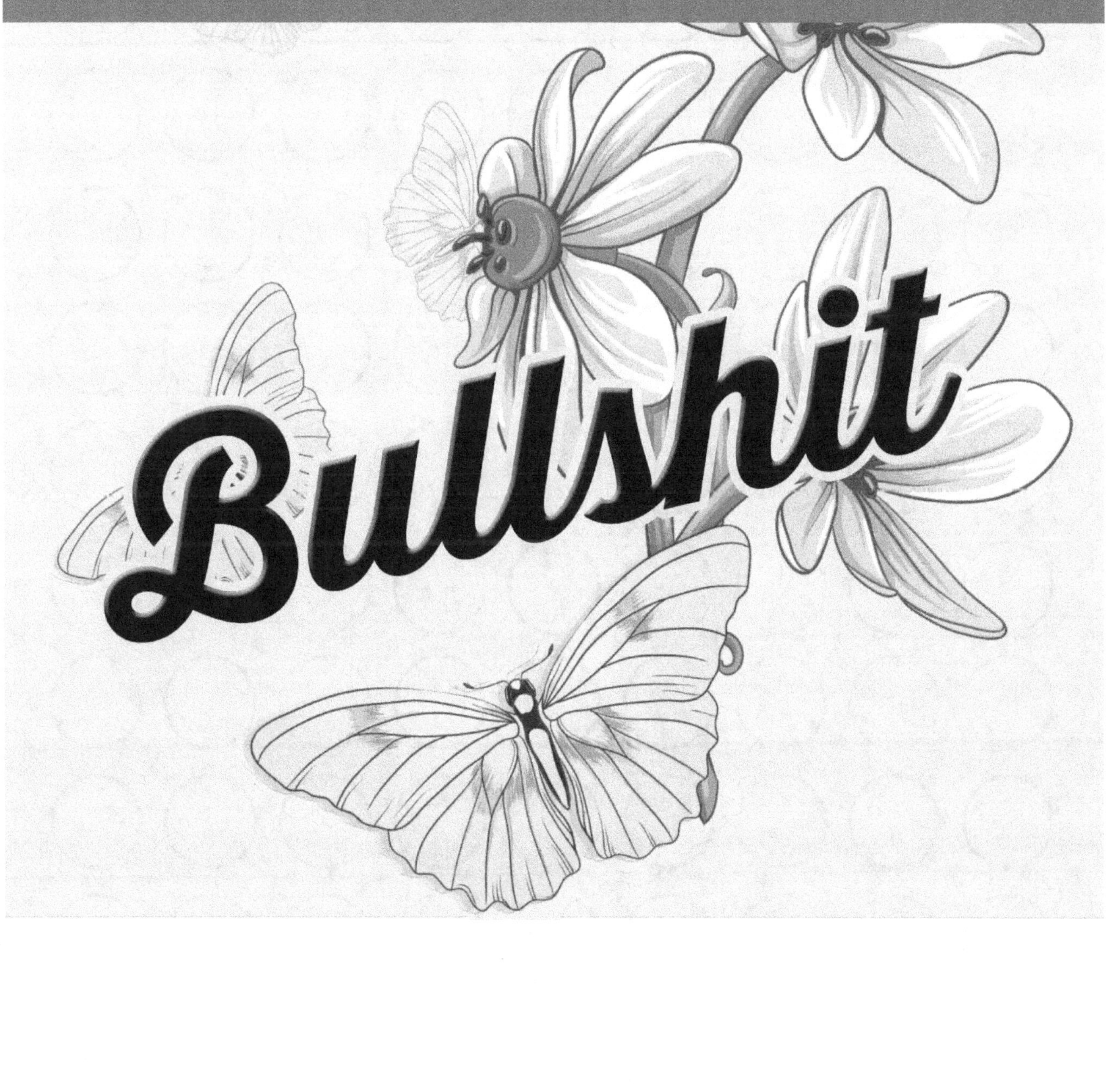

COLOR TEST PAGE

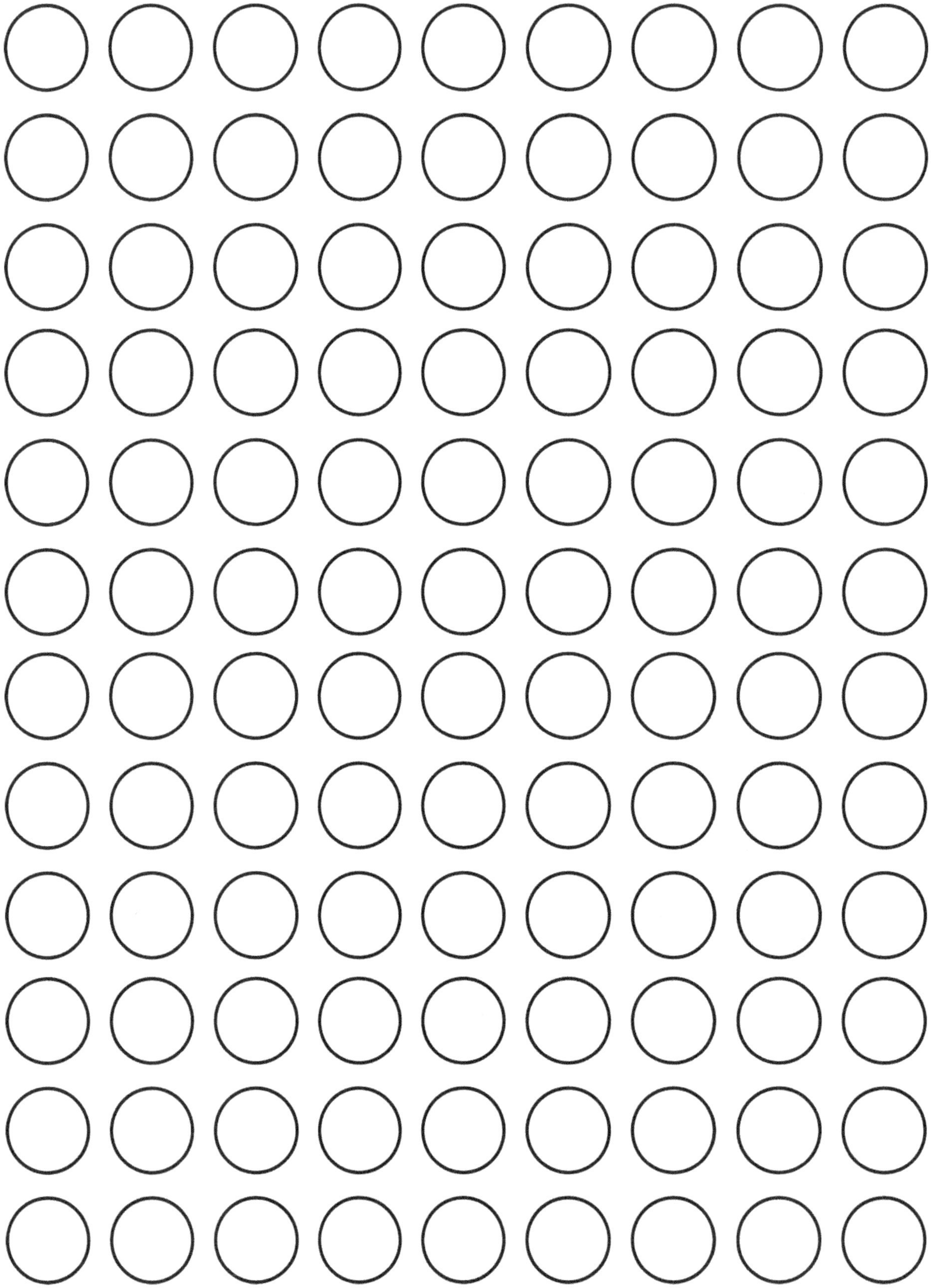

COLOR TEST PAGE

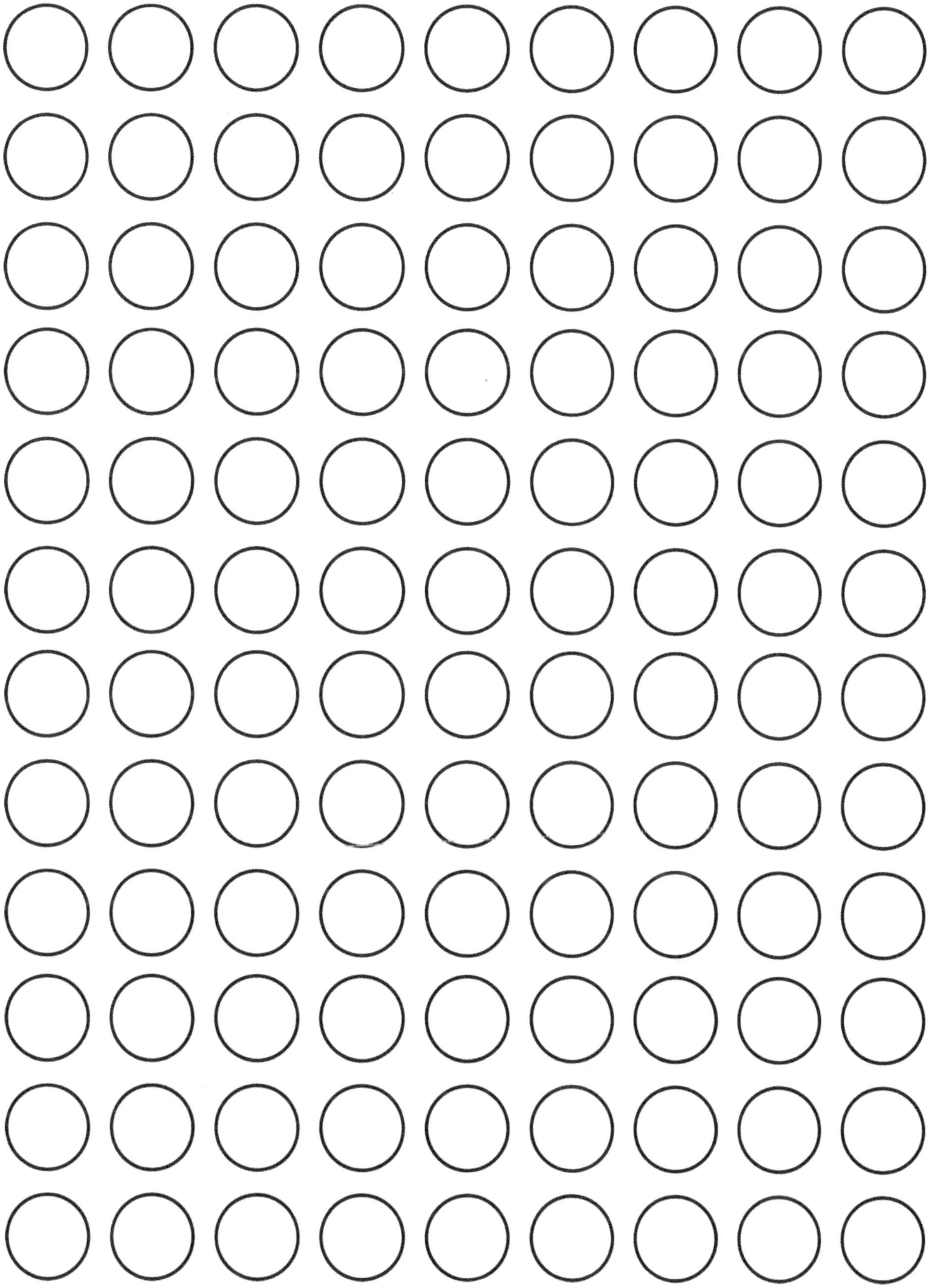

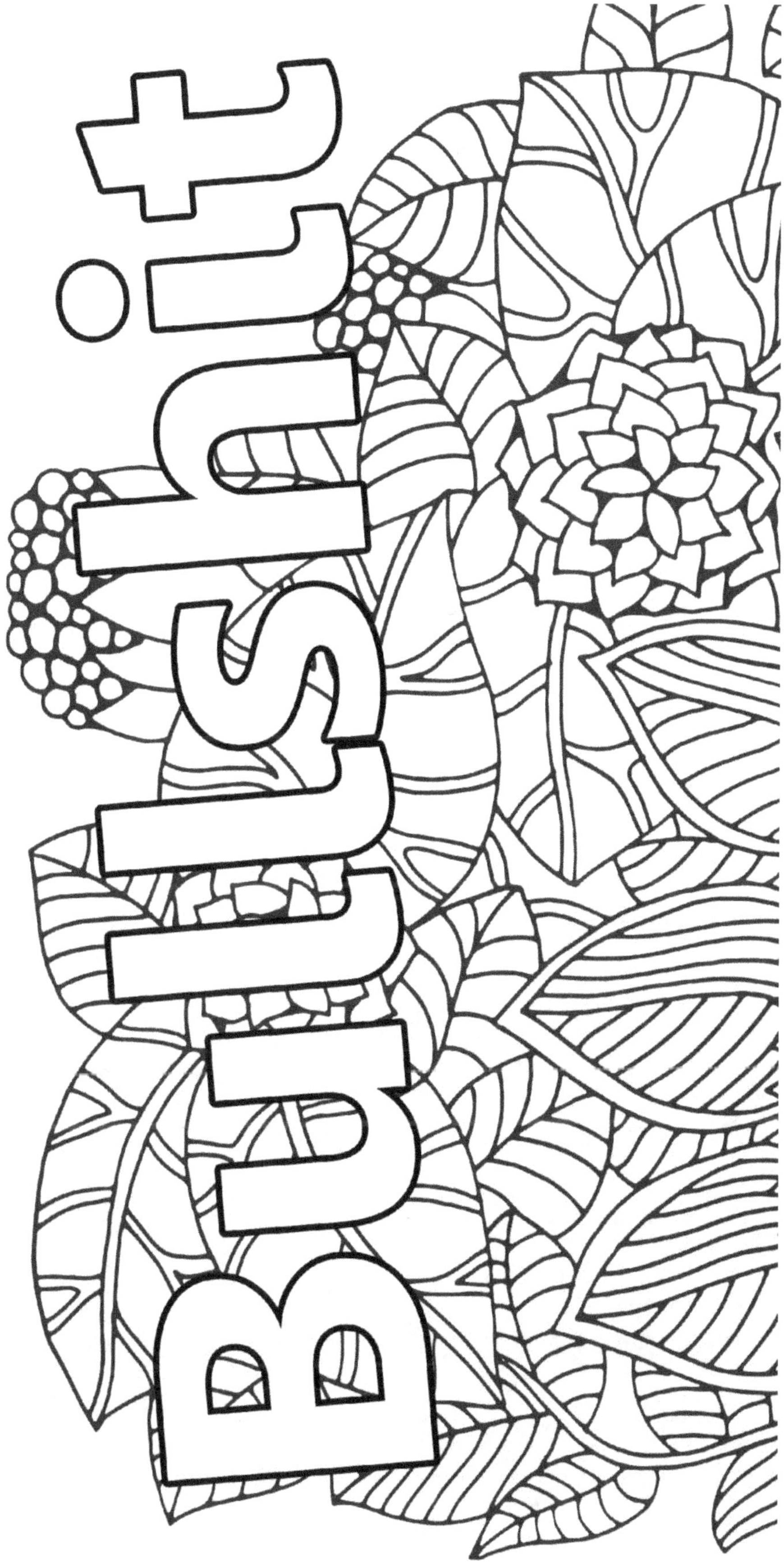
Bullshit

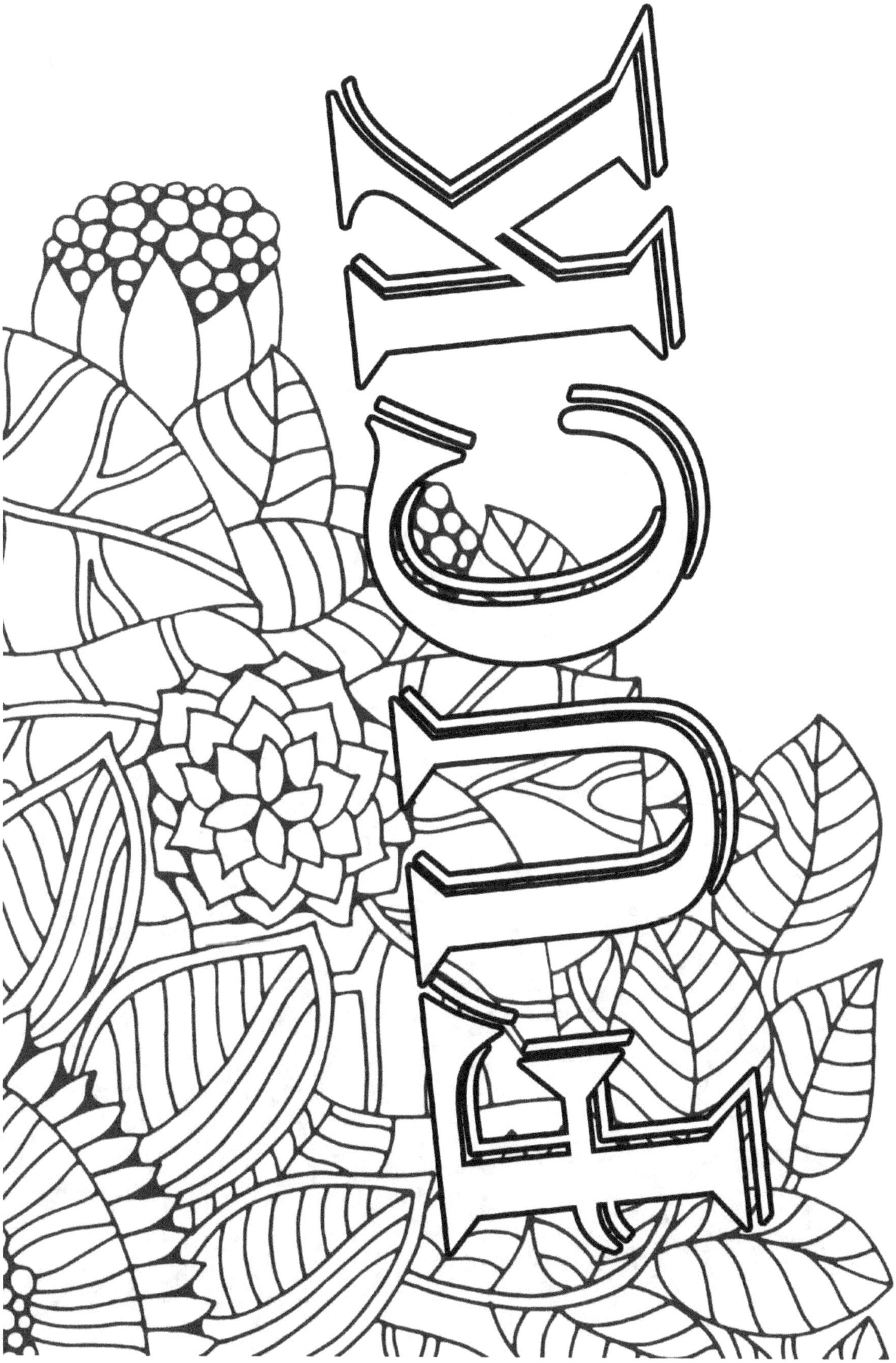
FUCK

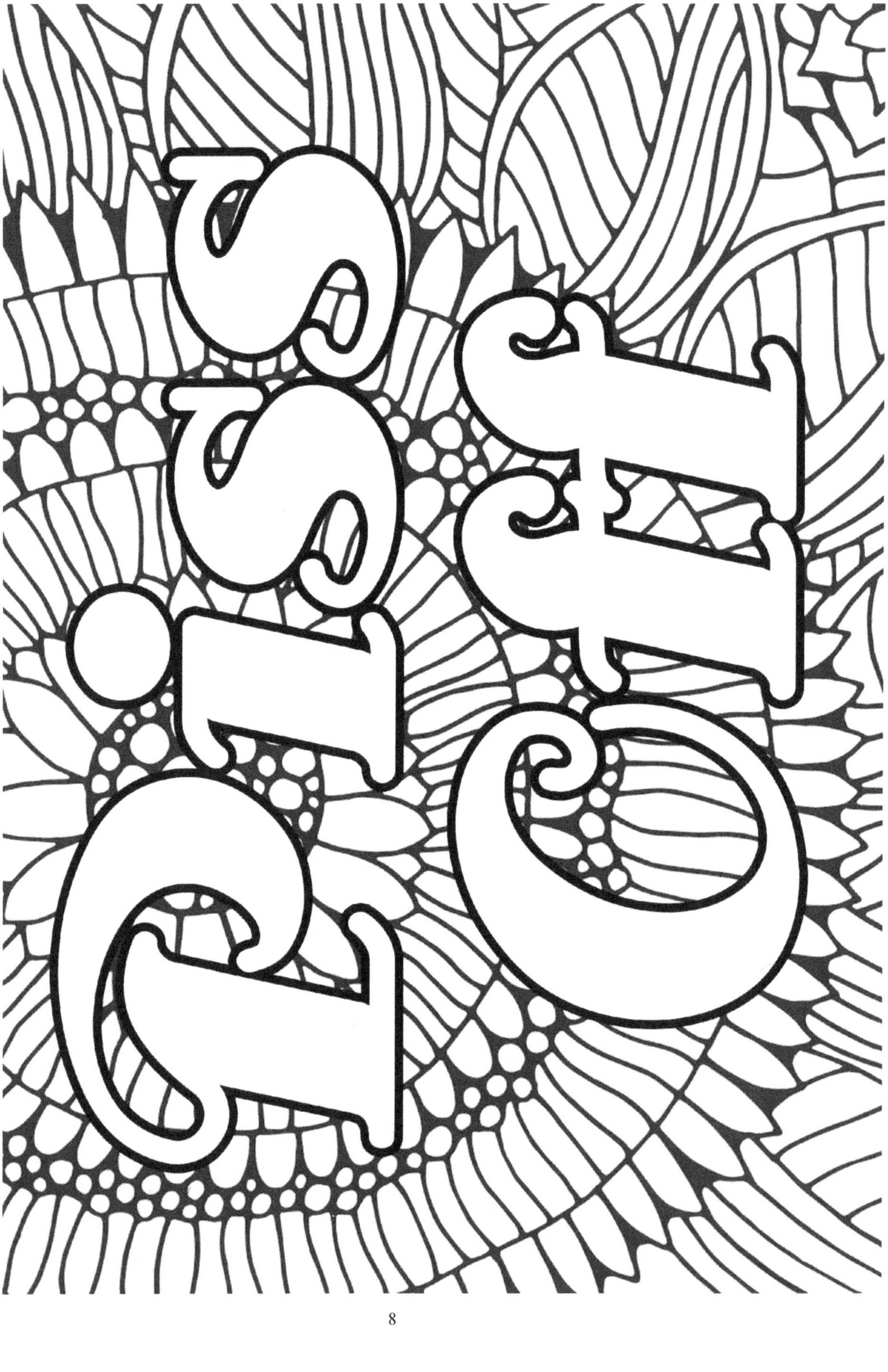
Piss Off

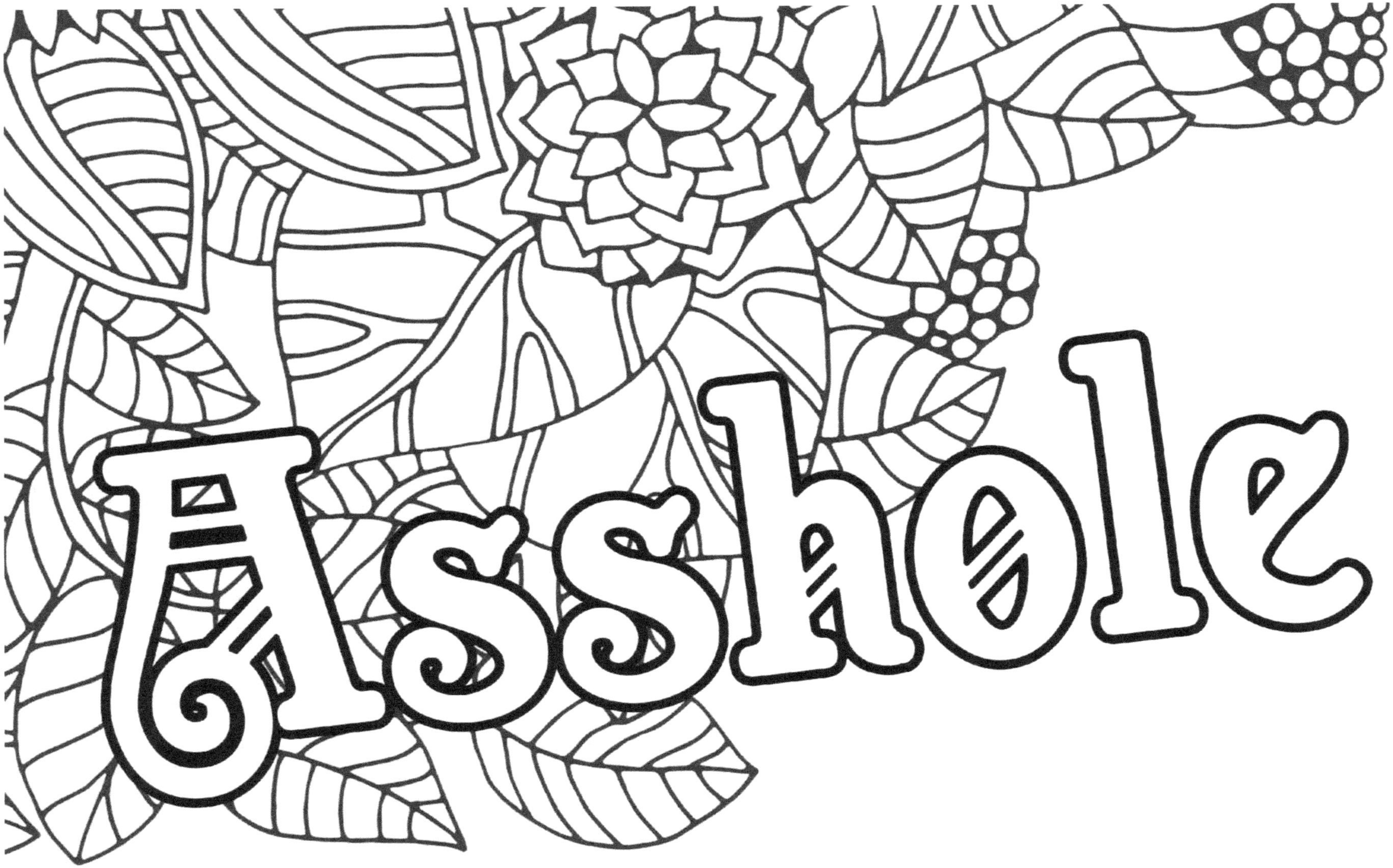
Asshole

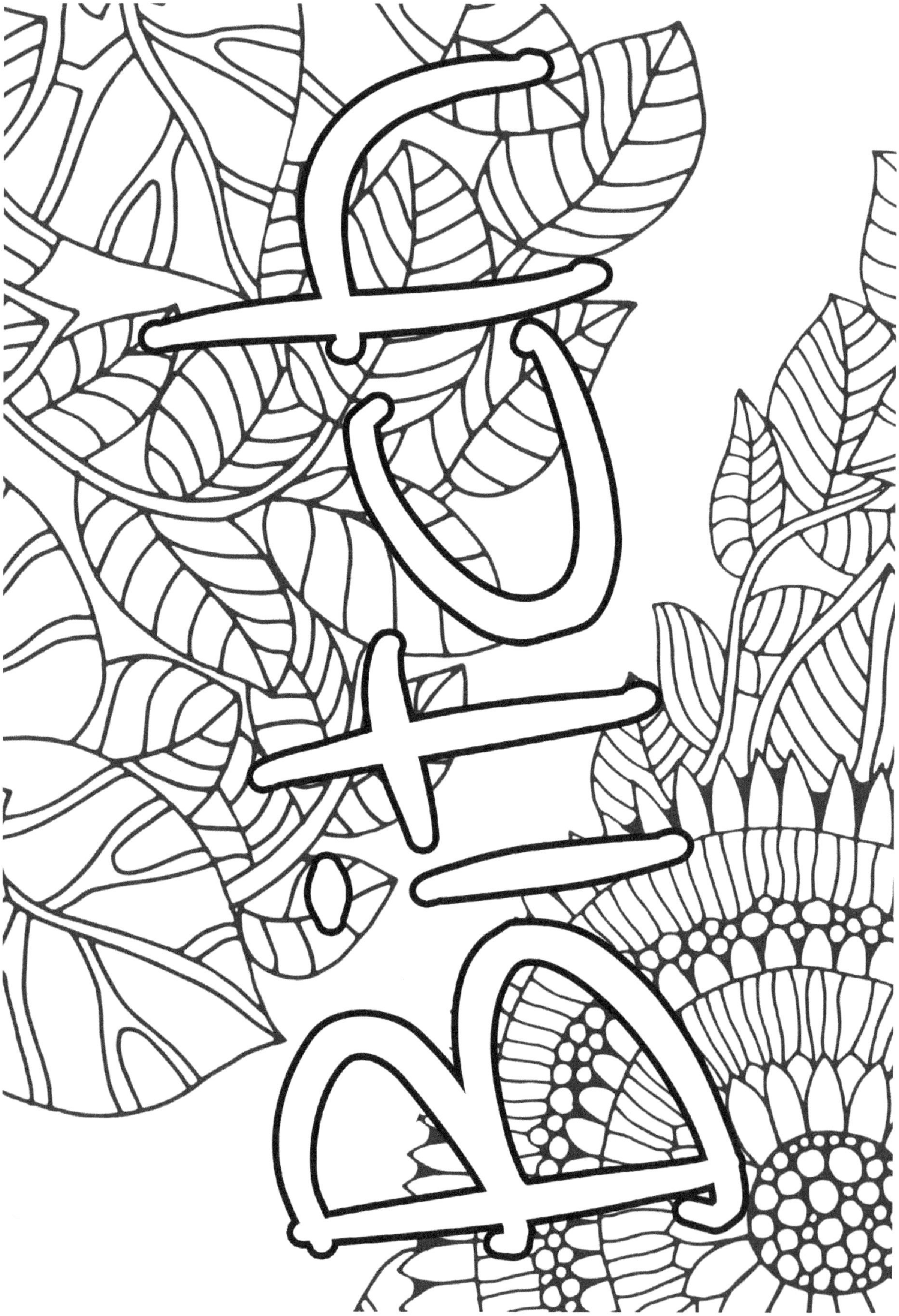
Bitch

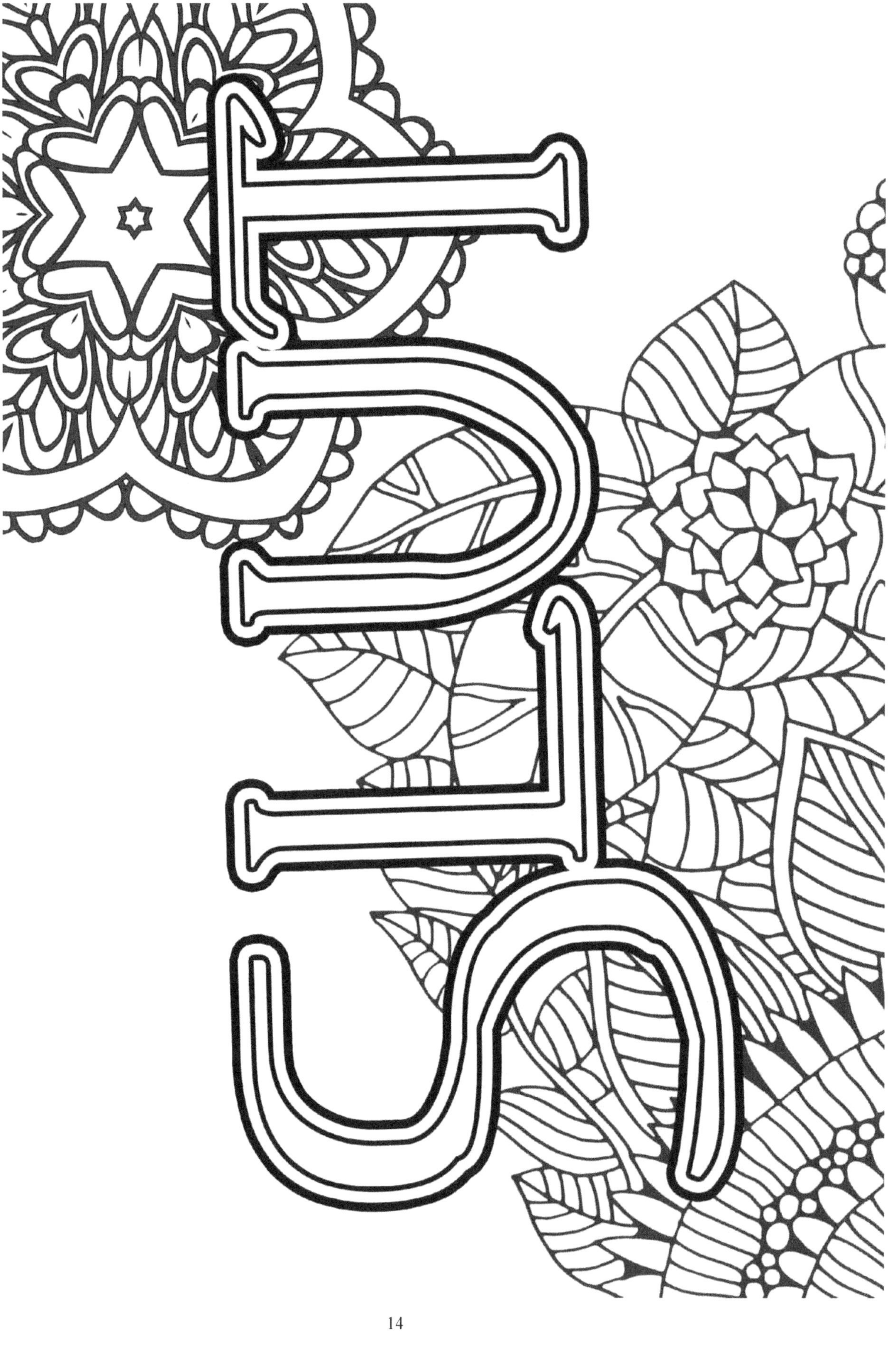
SLUT

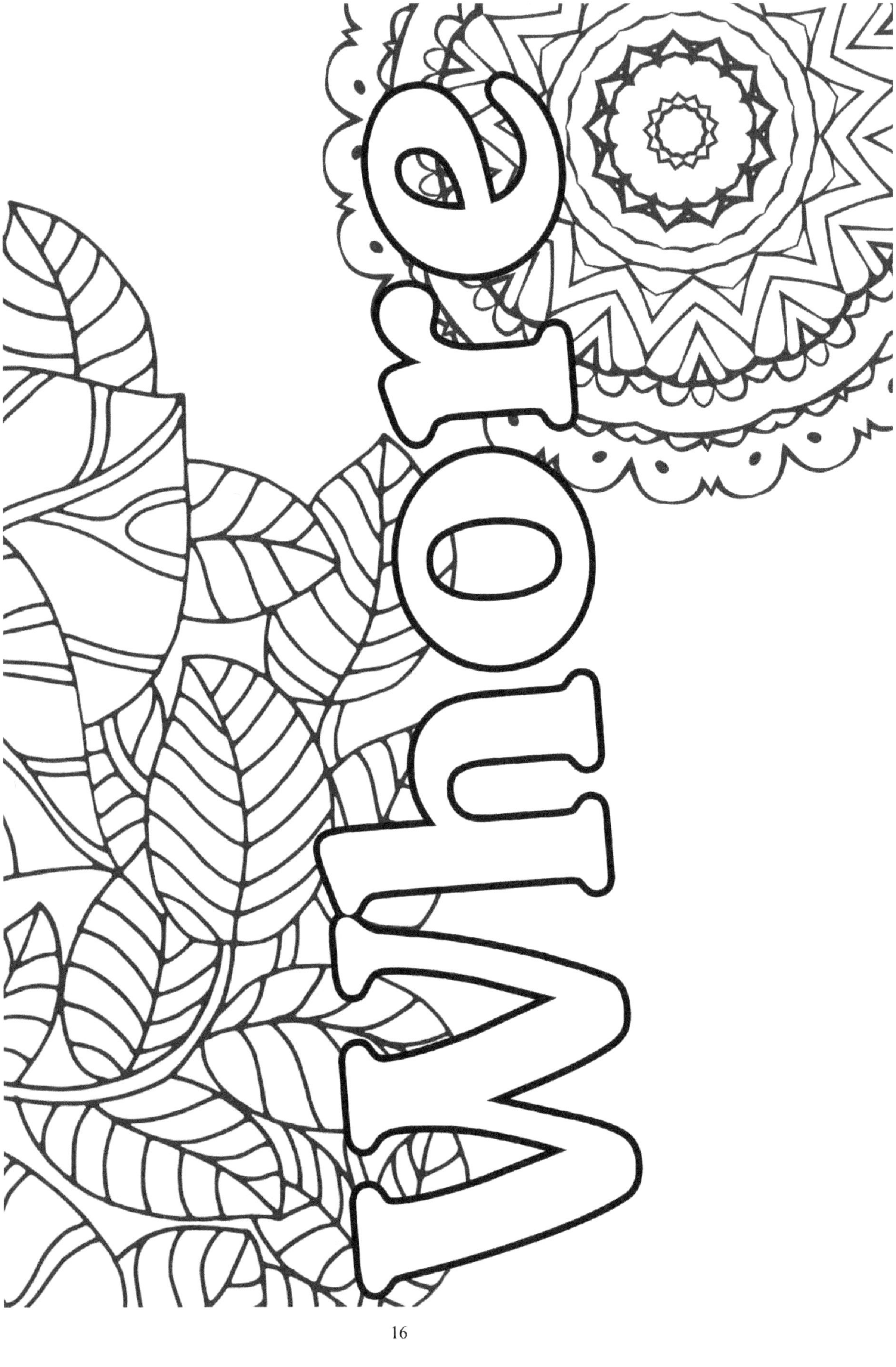
Whore

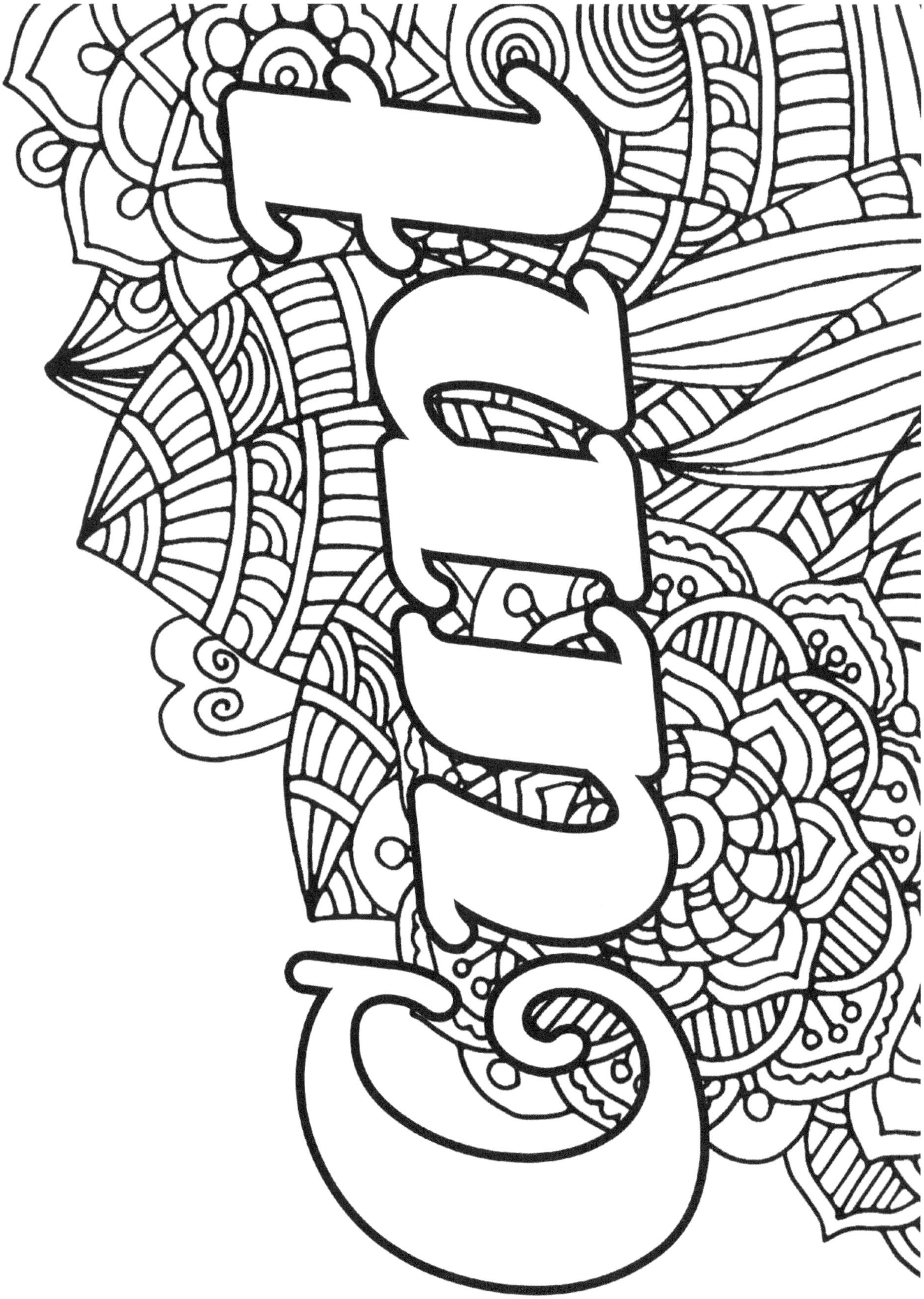
Cunt

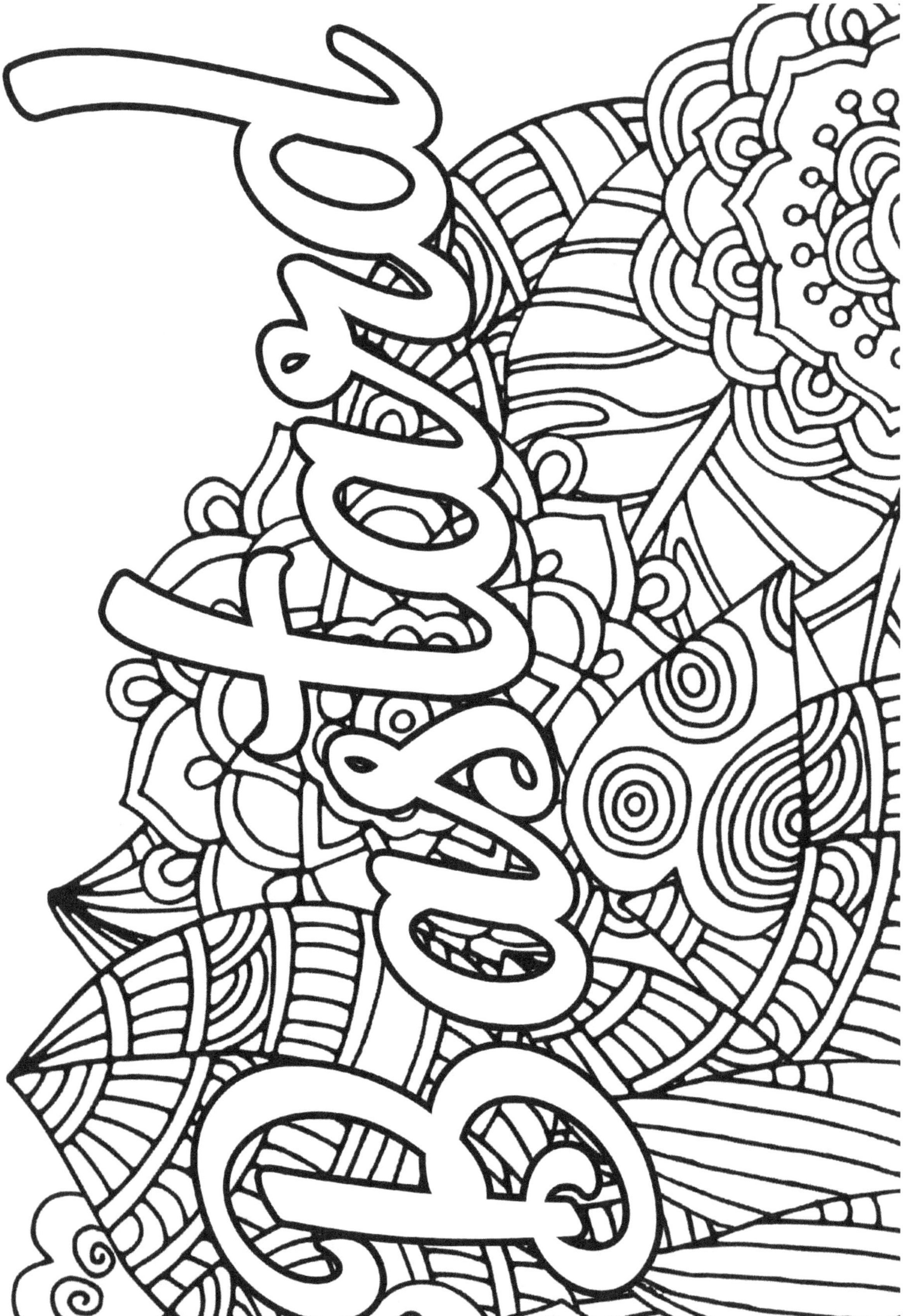
Bastard

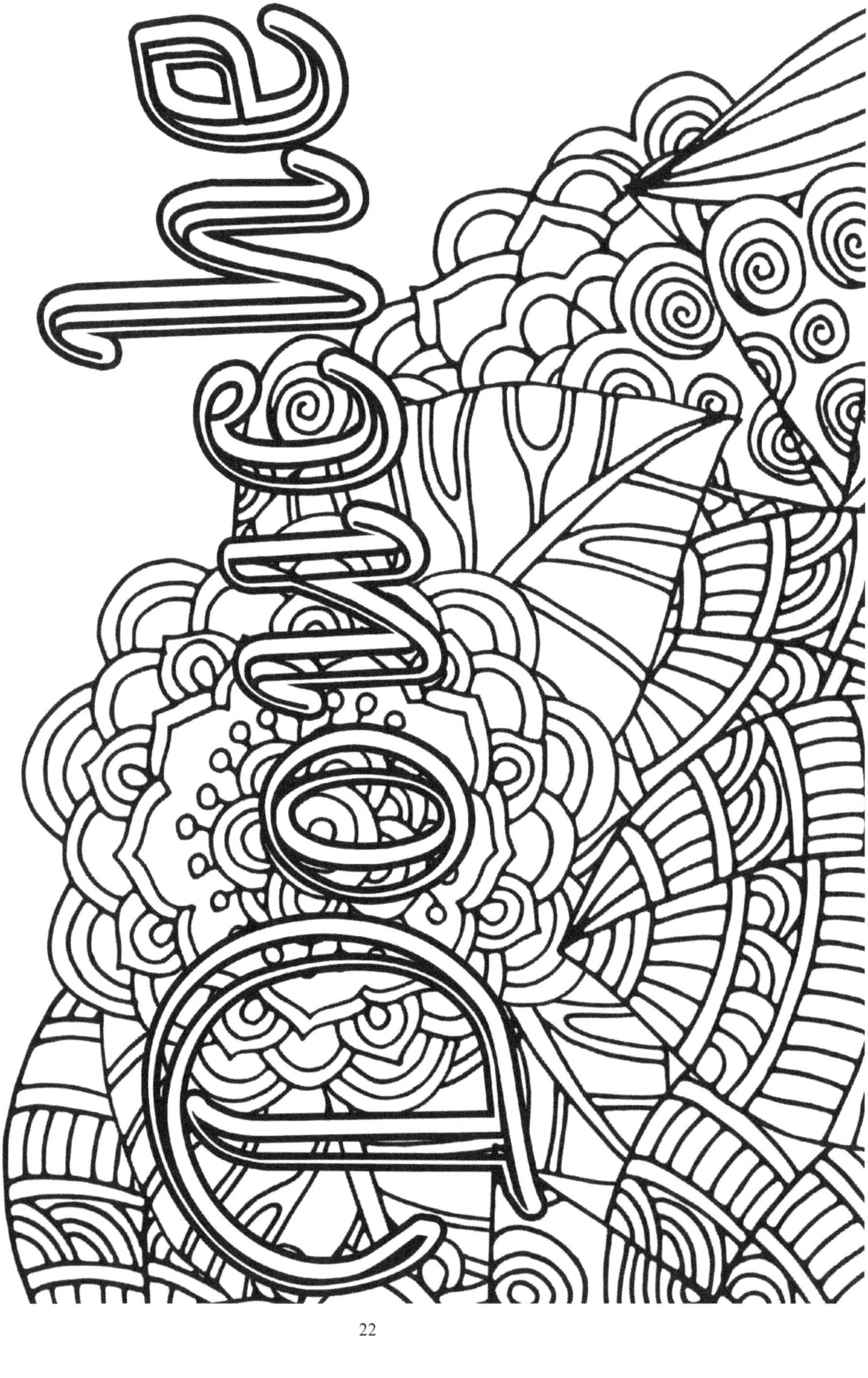
Douche

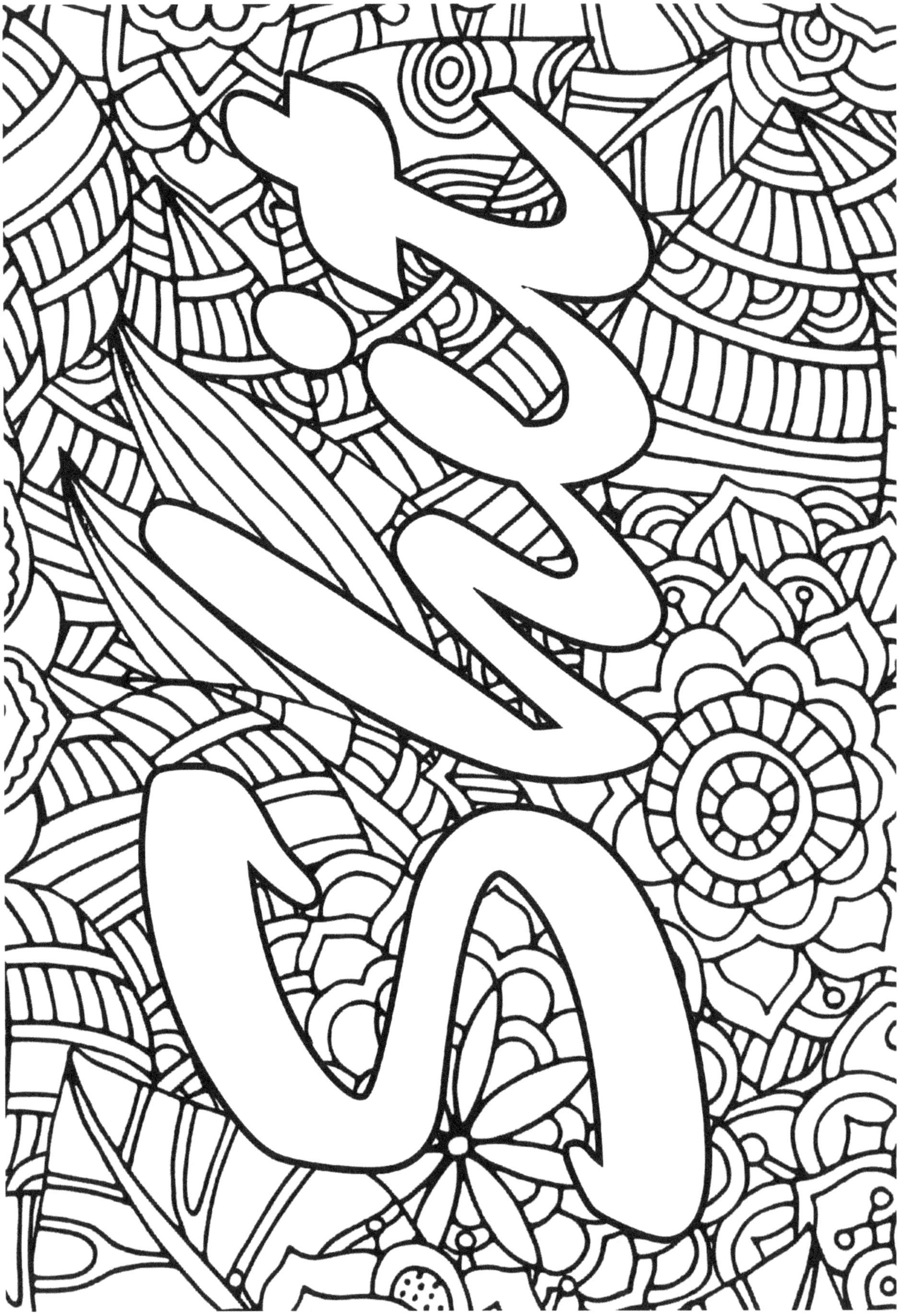

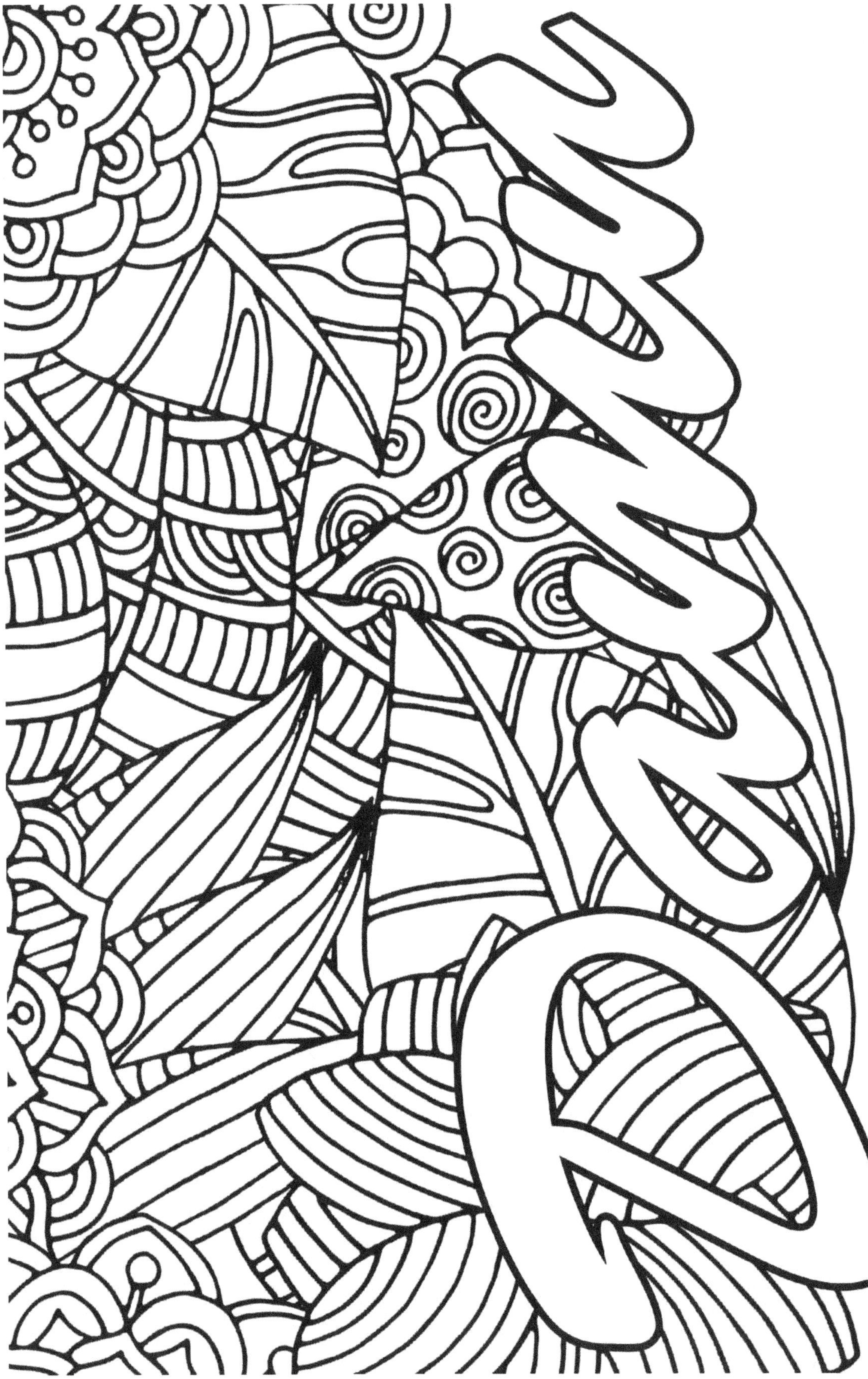
Damn

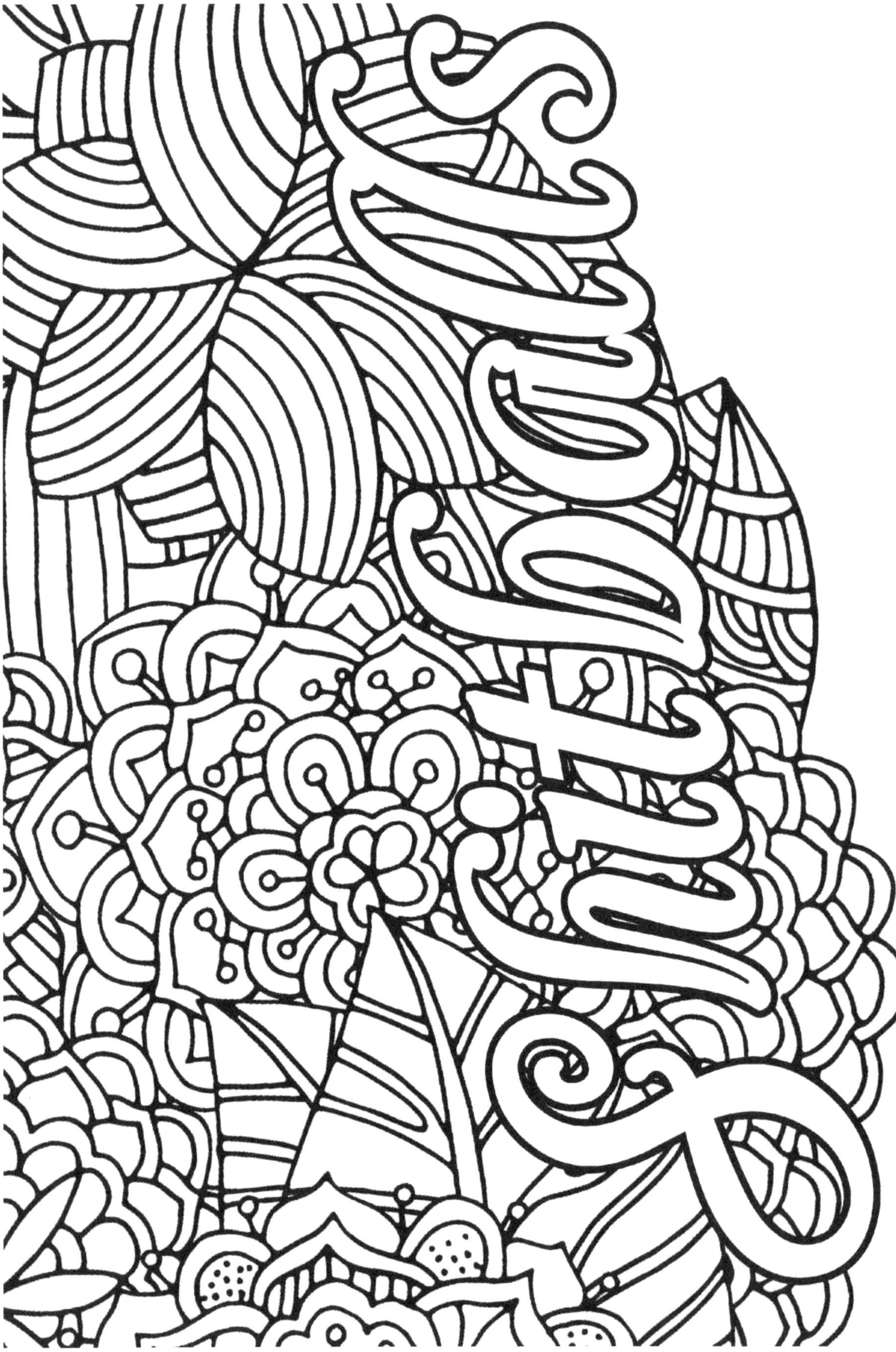
Shitballs

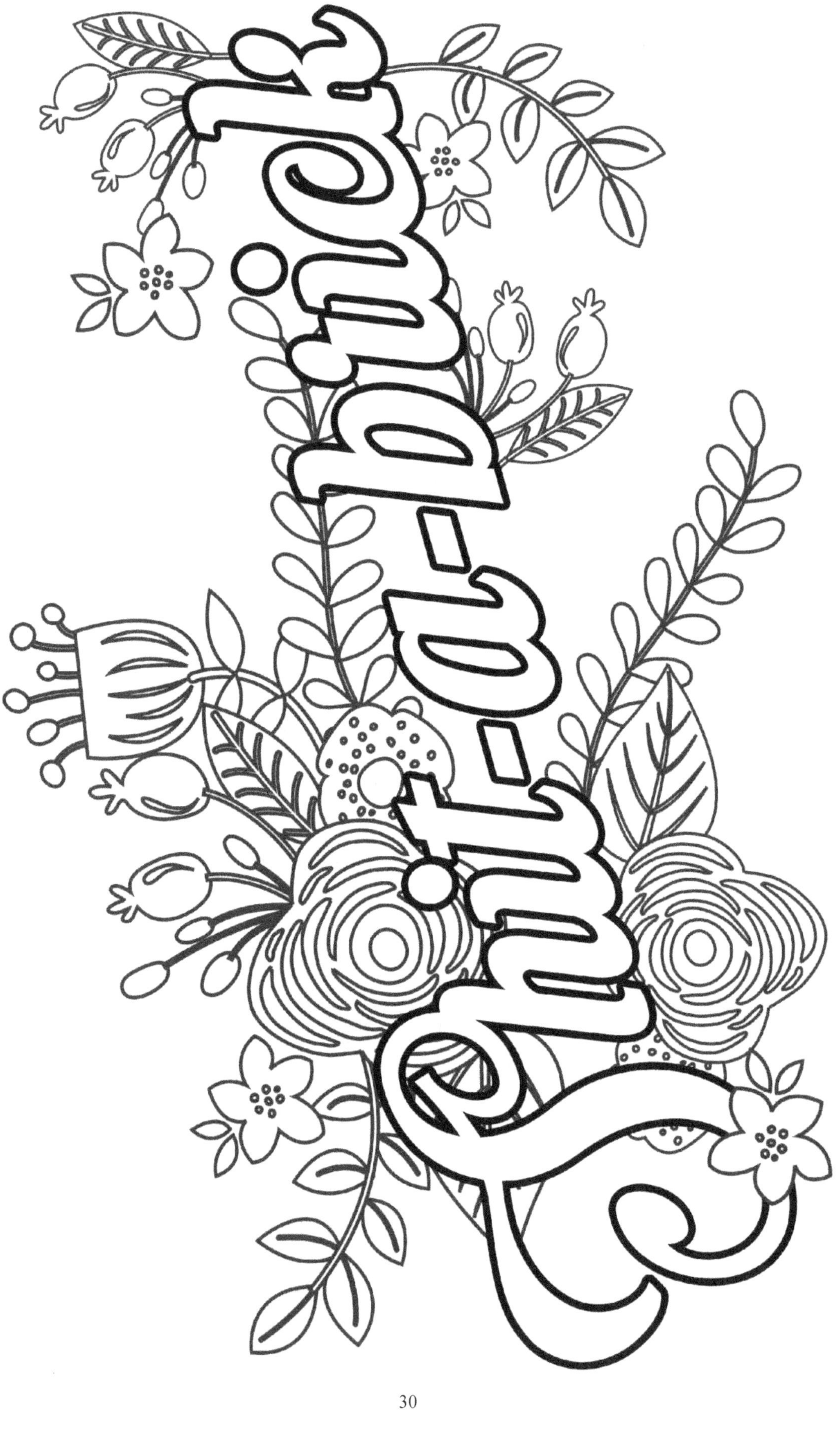
Shit-a-brick!

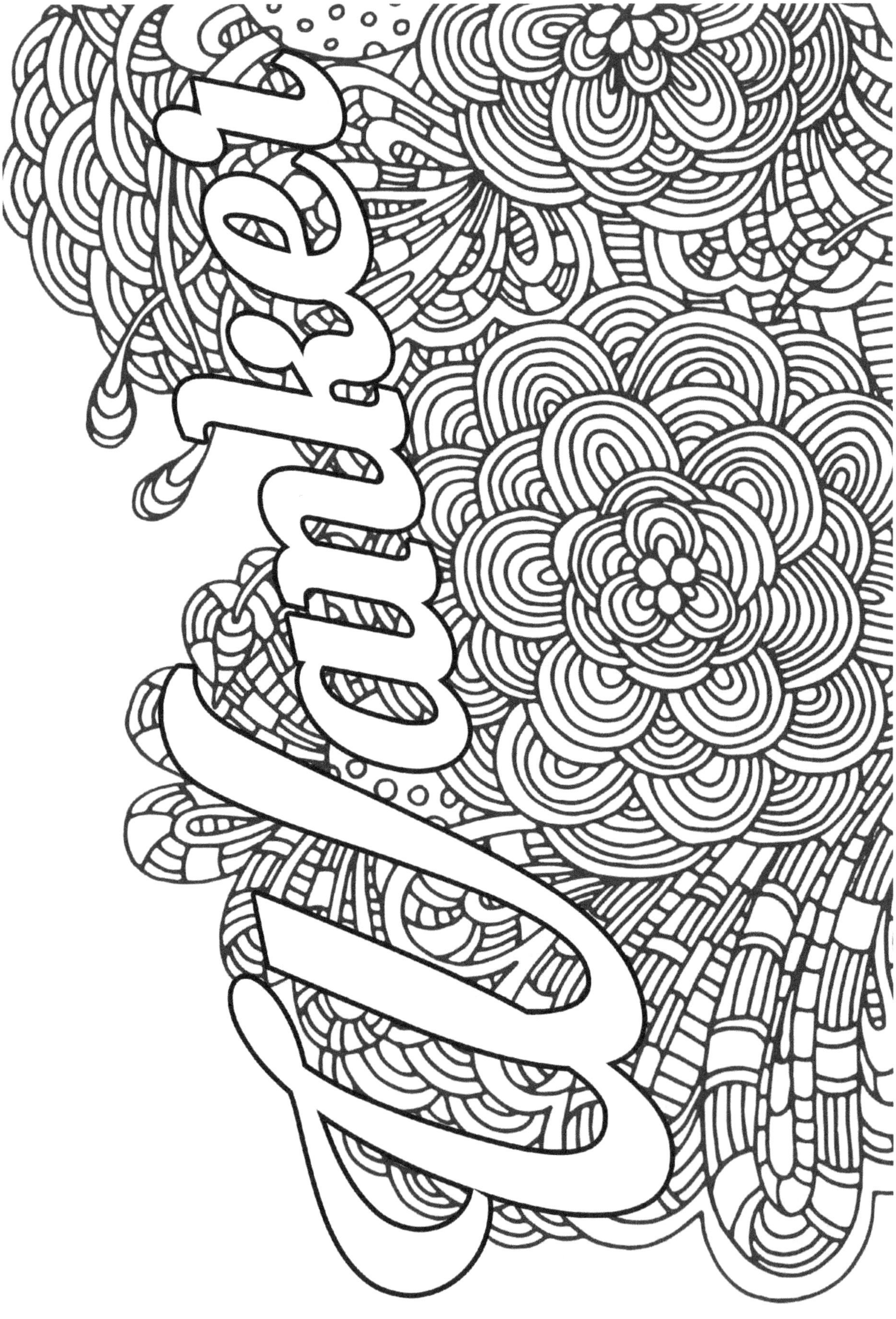
Murder

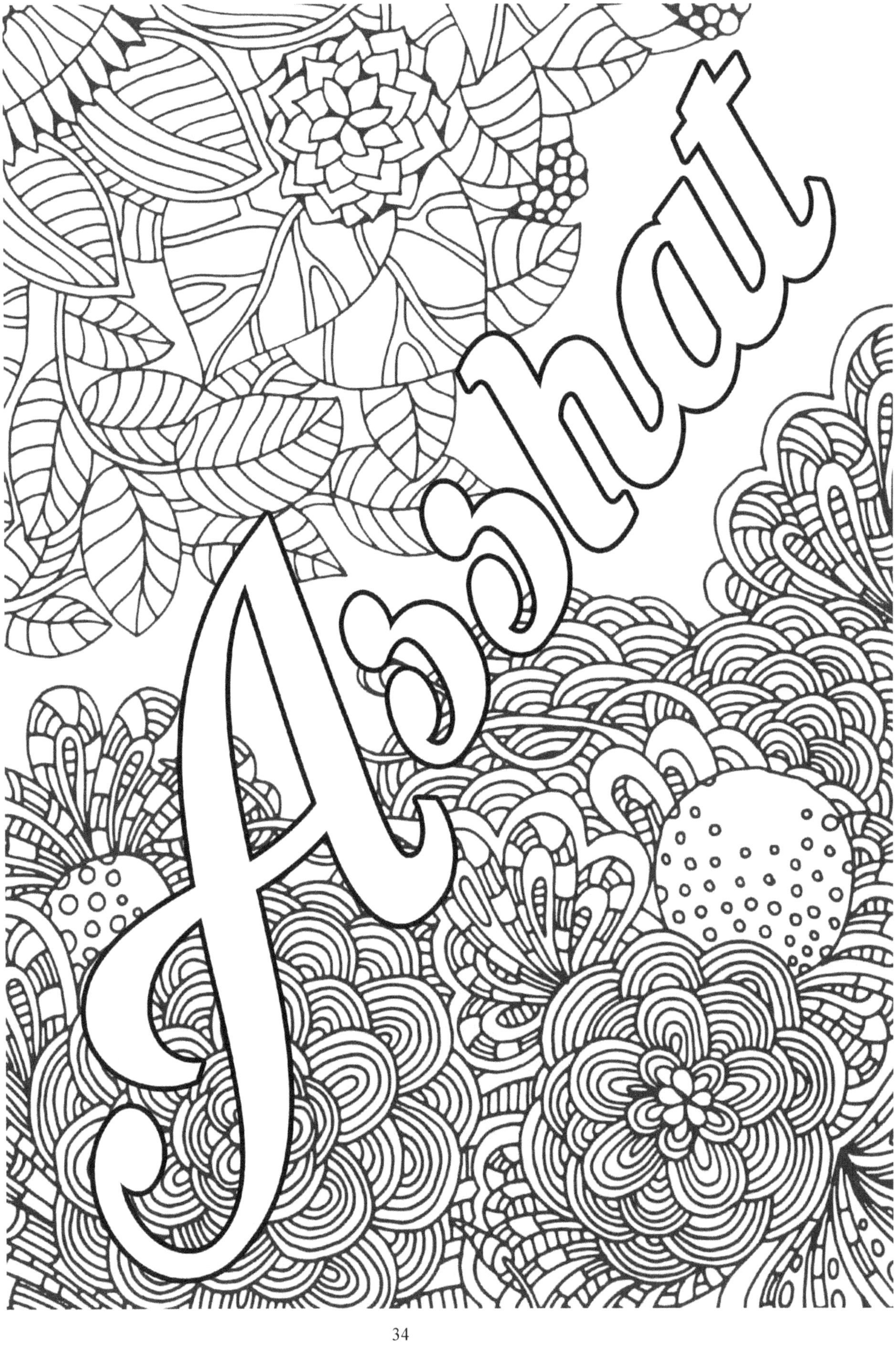
Asshat

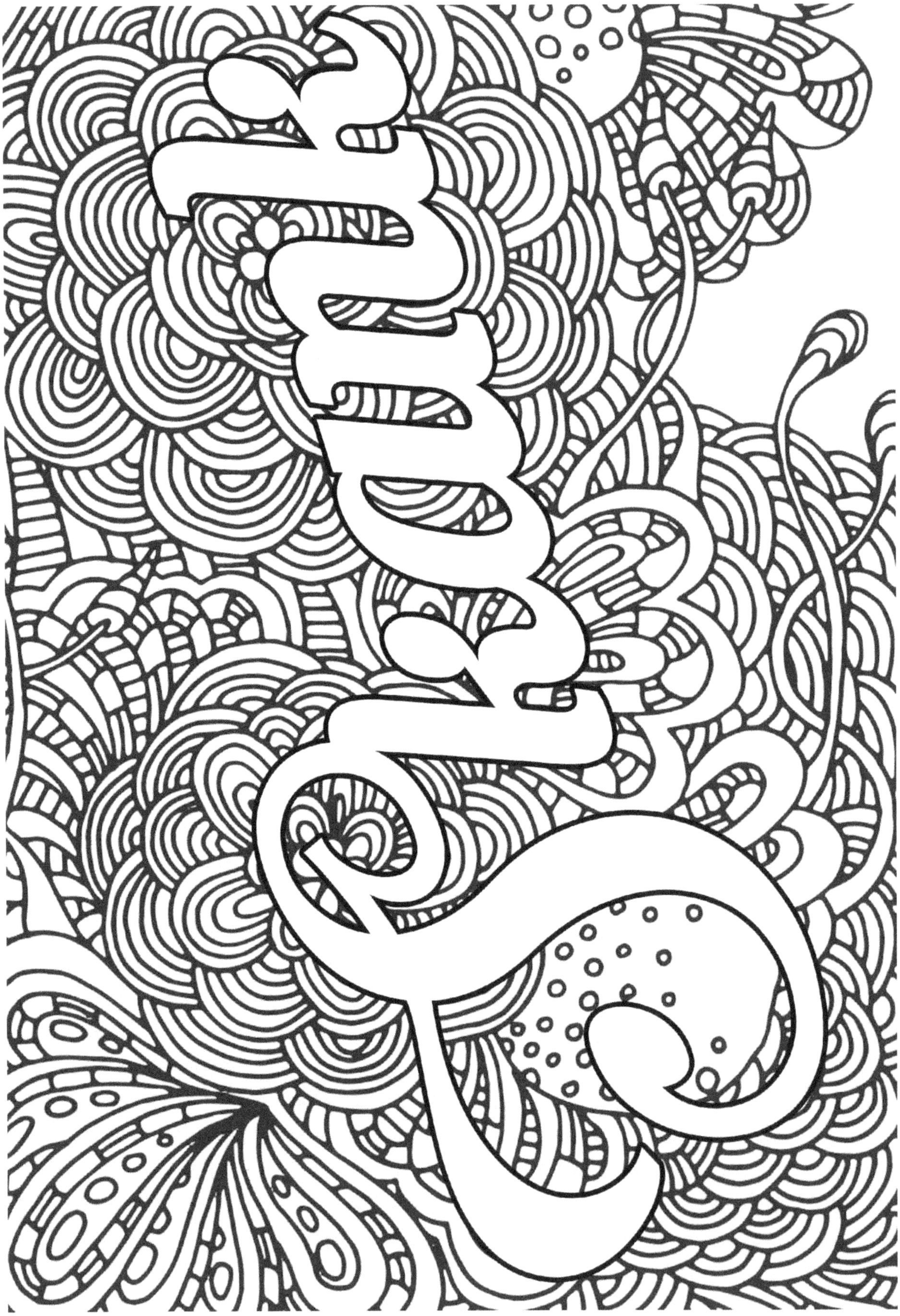
Skank

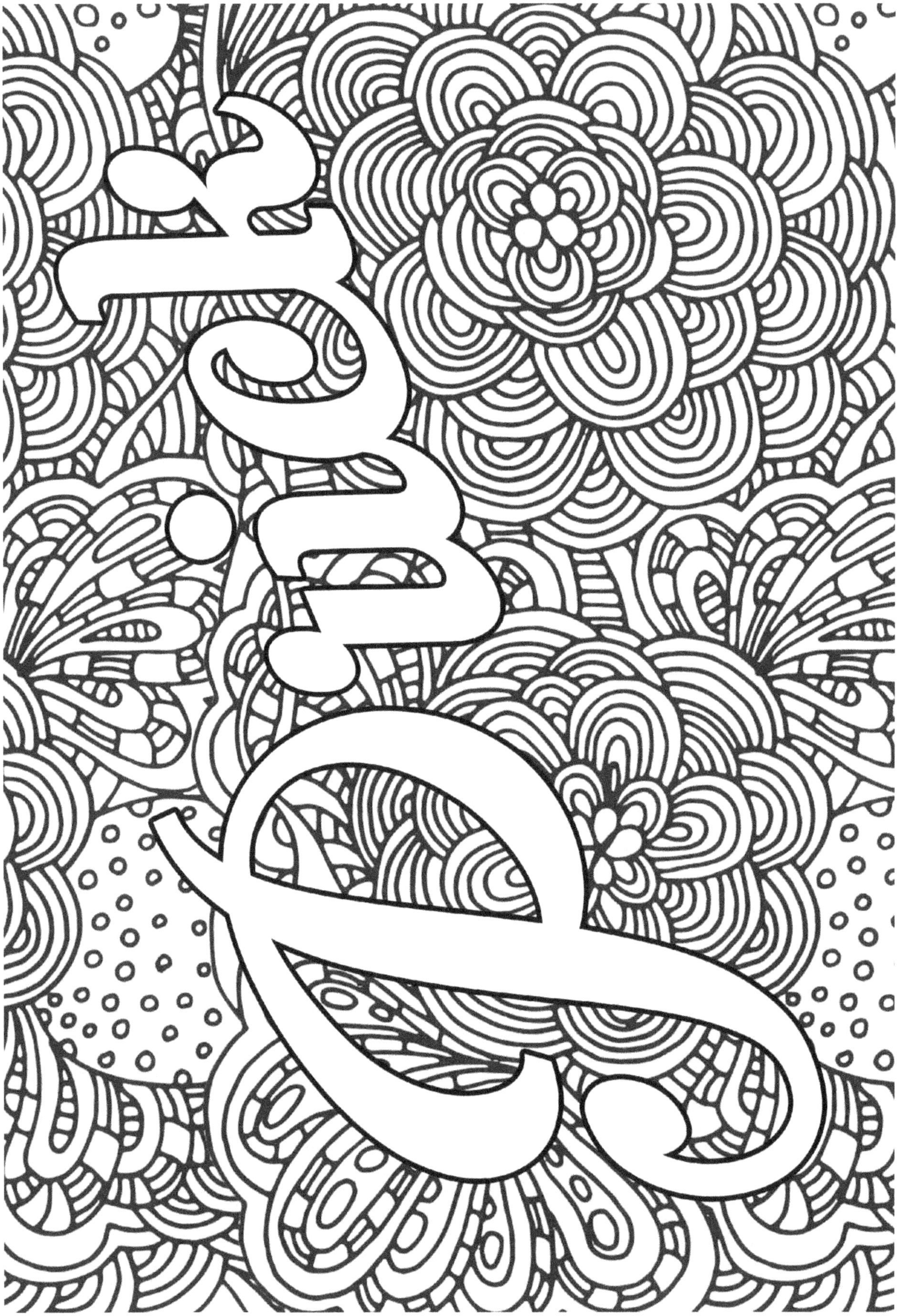
Fugly

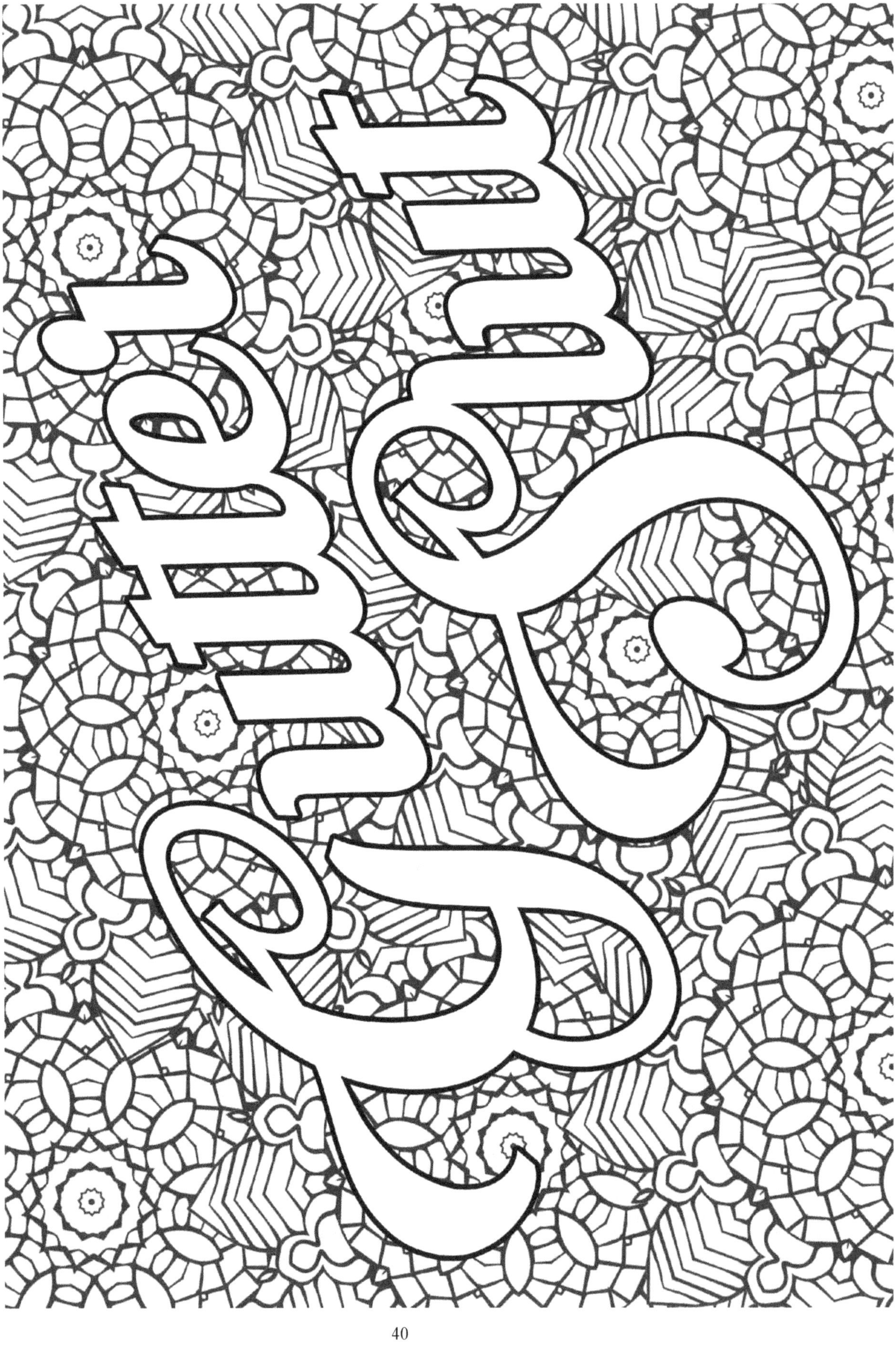
Gutter
Slut

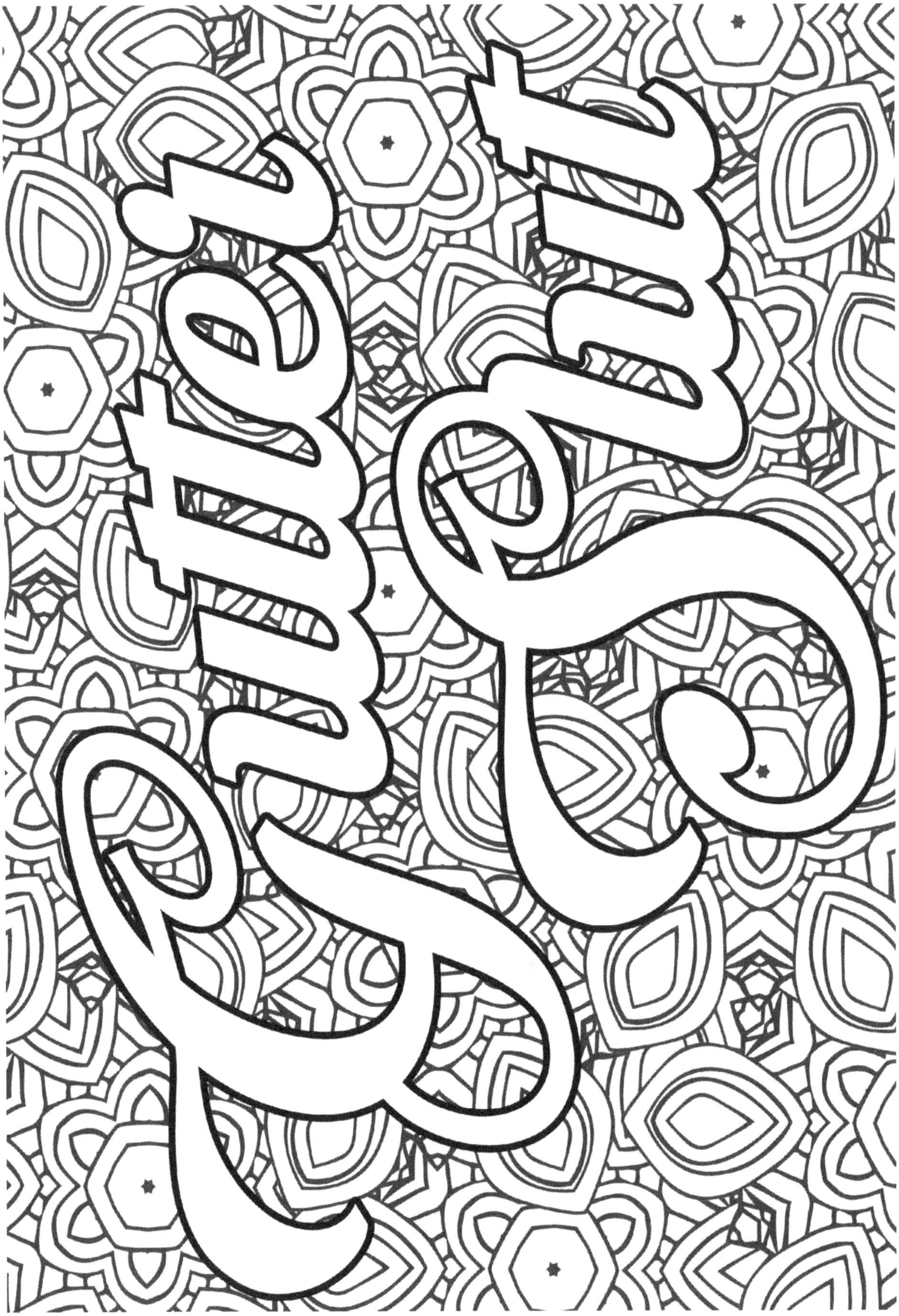
Gutter
Slut

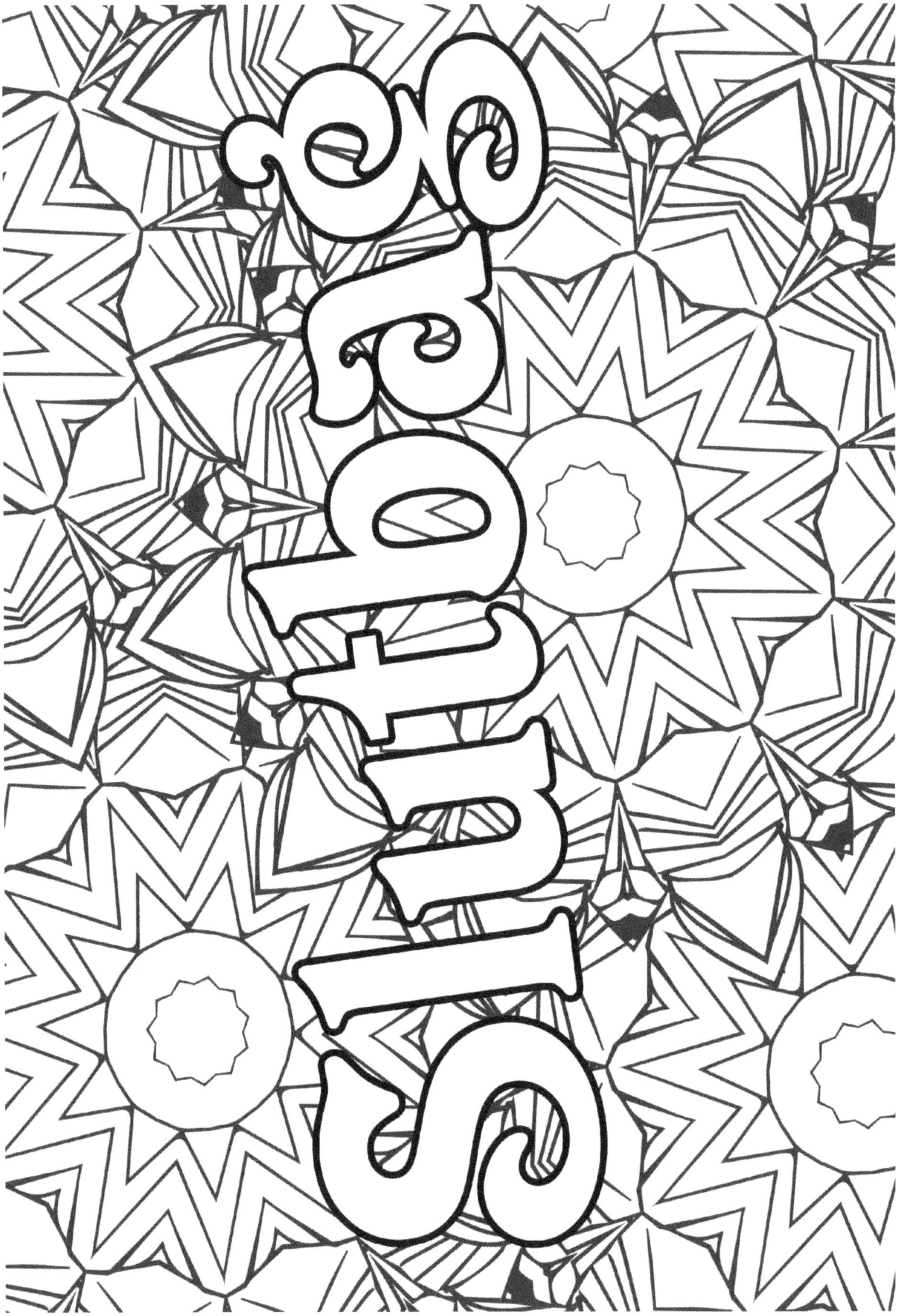
Slutbag

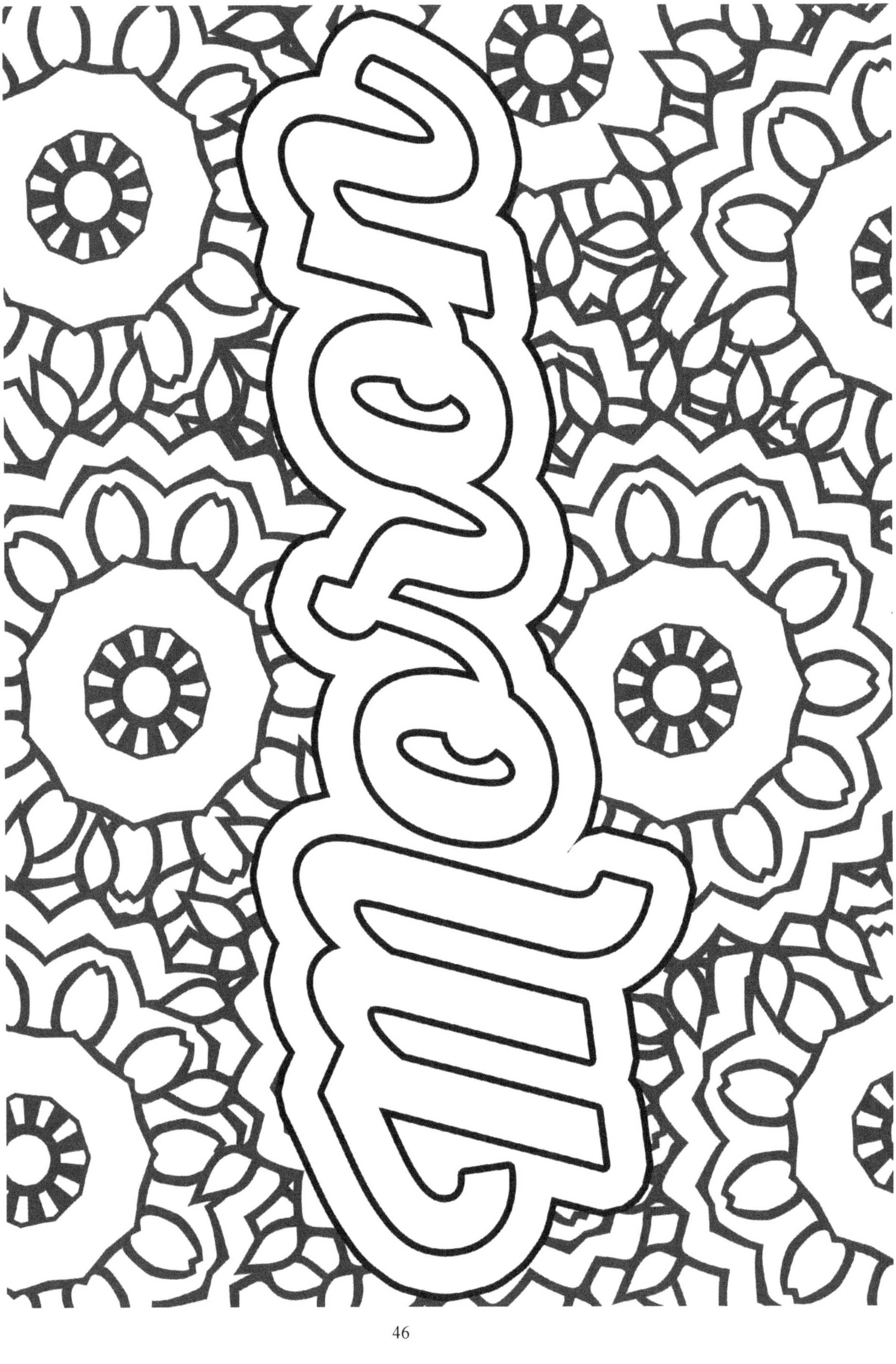
Moron

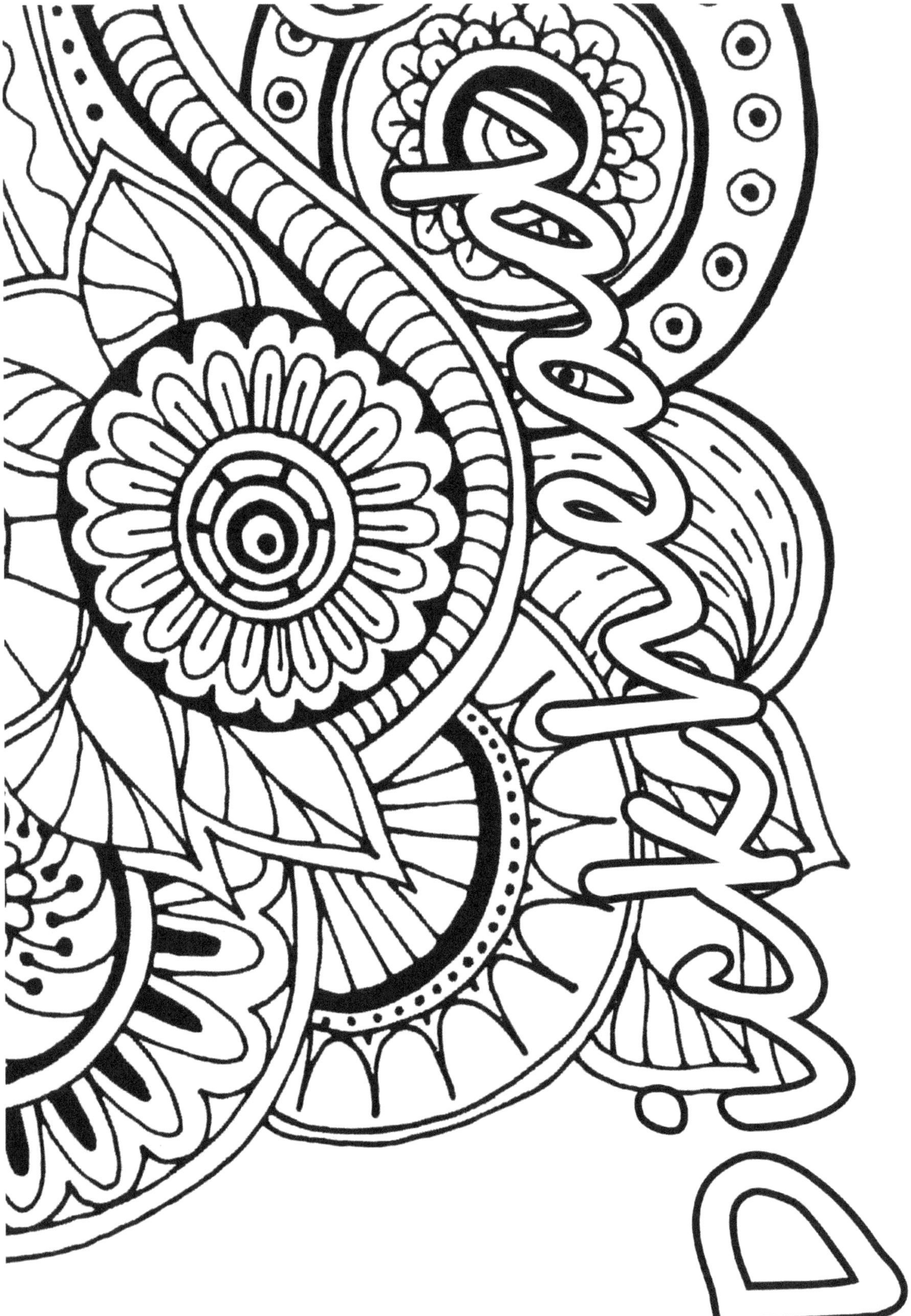

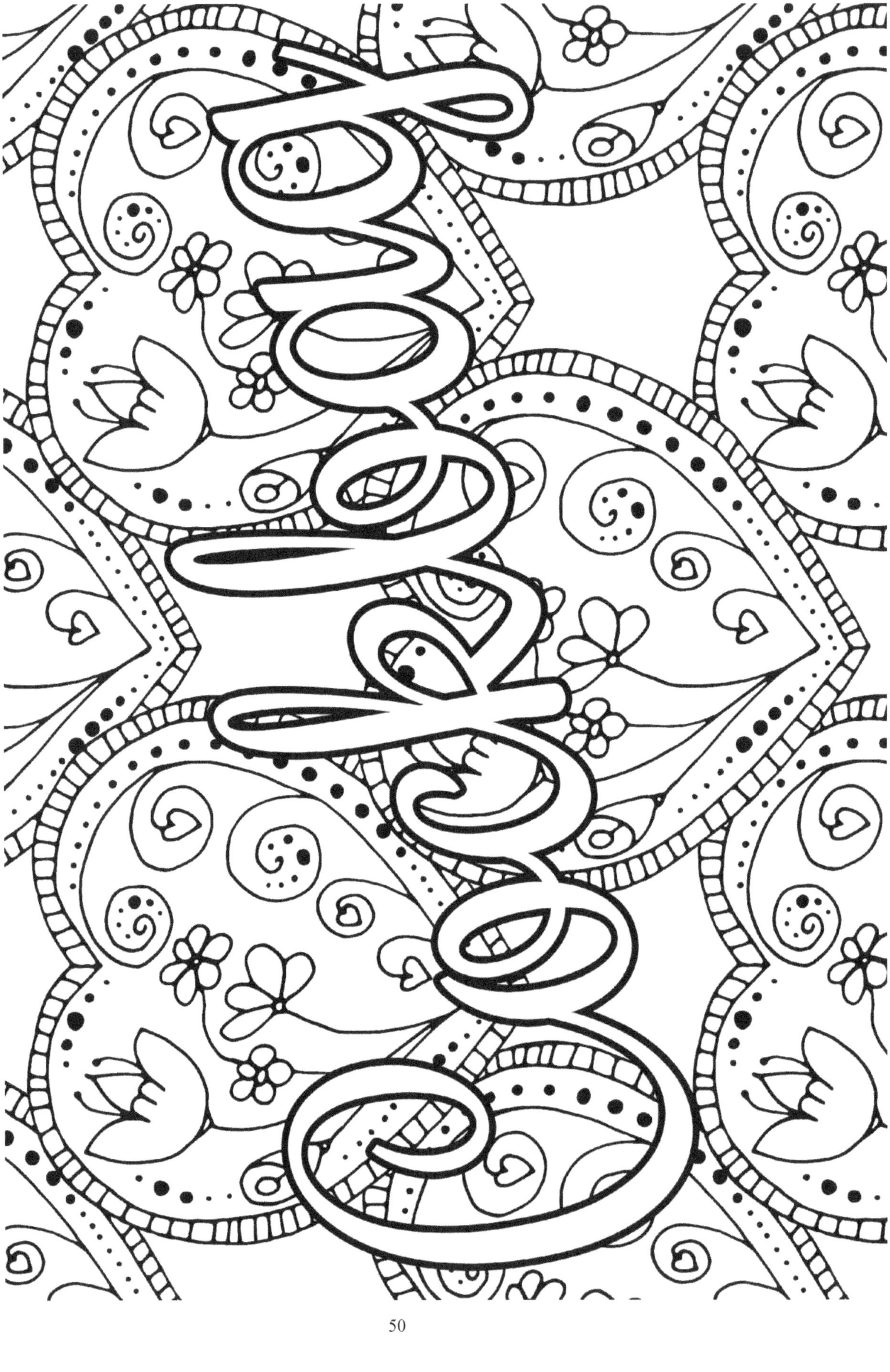
Cockbag